Liberty Blue
DINNERWARE

Liberty Blue
DINNERWARE

Debbie
&
Randy Coe

Schiffer Publishing Ltd ®

4880 Lower Valley Road, Atglen, PA 19310 USA

Designed by Bonnie M. Hensley
Cover design by Bruce M. Waters
Type set in Seavgull Hv BT/Zurich BT

ISBN: 0-7643-1543-9
Printed in China
1 2 3 4

Published by Schiffer Publishing Ltd.
4880 Lower Valley Road
Atglen, PA 19310
Phone: (610) 593-1777; Fax: (610) 593-2002
E-mail: Schifferbk@aol.com
Please visit our web site catalog at **www.schifferbooks.com**
We are always looking for people to write books on new and related subjects. If you have
an idea for a book, please contact us at the above address.

This book may be purchased from the publisher.
Include $3.95 for shipping. Please try your bookstore first.
You may write for a free catalog.

In Europe, Schiffer books are distributed by
Bushwood Books
6 Marksbury Ave. Kew Gardens
Surrey TW9 4JF England
Phone: 44 (0)20 8392-8585; Fax: 44 (0)20 8392-9876
E-mail: Bushwd@aol.com
Free postage in the UK. Europe: air mail at cost.
Please try your bookstore first.

Dedication

Dedicated to the men and women whose courageous actions have contributed to achieving our American freedoms. We are eternally grateful for the sacrifices they made to establish our great nation.

Contents

Acknowledgements

We would like to thank Donna & Ron Miller and Barbara & Harlan Parsons for generously sharing their Liberty Blue collections with us and for furnishing information for this book. We greatly appreciate all they did. Our daughters, Myra and Tara· Coe, helped with all the proof reading. We greatly appreciate all their other help in getting many things done to assist us in this project. We love you both, lots! We really appreciate all the help Jim Yaple and his fellow members of the Lewis and Clark Chapter of the Sons of the American Revolution gave us. They were a wonderful source of information in providing accurate historical facts about the scenes. The staff at the *Hillsboro Argus* was absolutely wonderful in locating the particular newspapers we needed. They were glad to be of assistance even though they were busy meeting their own deadlines. Suburban Photo, in Beaverton, Oregon, has continued to provide great customer service. Their staff is always friendly and efficient. Our editor, Nancy Schiffer, has been terrific in always being ready to help with any problems or questions. No matter when, she is accessible to us. She really is one super lady! We appreciate everyone who helped with this project.

Introduction

Now that a quarter century has passed since the first Liberty Blue dinnerware was made, many people have become interested in collecting this patriotic and attractive service. Many who have purchased Liberty Blue pieces want more information about this pattern. The standard question is always, "Why isn't there a book on Liberty Blue?"

To address the needs of collectors, we have made a detailed listing of all the known pieces. Sizes are given for each piece. Since the various pieces picture historic scenes, we have provided background information about that scene. There is also a listing of pieces that could be used with the Liberty Blue. Original ads and brochures have also been used.

Our initial listing came from the Benjamin Franklin brochures. As we photographed the collections, more pieces were added to the list. Since there were additional pieces made for the grocery store promotions, there could be other pieces that we haven't listed. Please let us know about any new discovery. We encourage everyone to give us feedback about this book.

Back - Large size oval turkey platter, 20" long with signing of the Declaration of Independence scene. **Center left** - Mug, Hot Chocolate, 3.75" tall with Mount Vernon scene. **Center Right** - Coaster 4" diameter with George Washington at Valley Forge scene. **Front left** - Gravy boat liner, 7.9" long with Governors House scene and Gravy boat, 7.75" long with Lafayette landing at West Point scene. **Front center** - Soup tureen with cover, 8" tall by 13" wide with Boston Tea Party scene on cover and with Minutemen scene on bottom. **Front right** - Name plate, 2.25" by 3.75" all white.

Back - Original box in which the basic place setting was packaged. **Front left** - Dinner plate, 9.75" diameter with Independence Hall scene. **Front center** - Bread and butter plate, 5.75" diameter with Monticello scene. **Front right** - Coffee cup, 2.75" tall with Paul Revere scene and saucer, 5.75" diameter with Old North Church scene.

Measurements

All measurements given are actual ones. Bowls, butter dish, coasters, gravy boat & liner, plates, platters and saucer are measured according to their diameter or length, depending on whether they are round or oblong. Creamer, cup, mug, pitcher, soup tureen, sugar and teapot are measured by height; then liquid measure is given. Shakers are measured by height only.

Value Guide

Values are given for MINT CONDITION only. Items that are chipped, cracked or scratched will bring substantially less than the given price. Any staining will also reduce the value. There are, of course, differences in the prices across different regions. Some pieces may be more prevalent in one area while another area may have a shortage of items. All values have been derived from several sources. Remember, the ultimate decision for value rests with the collector who determines what they are willing to pay for an item. Neither the authors nor the publisher assumes any responsibility for transactions that may occur because of this book.

Chapter 1

Background and History

The Benjamin Franklin Federal Savings and Loan was a large financial institution in the Pacific Northwest. It was established in 1925 and the first office opened in Portland, Oregon. In order to commemorate their 50th anniversary in 1975, the Board of Directors looked for something special to offer their account holders. They contacted the Enoch Wedgwood Company, located in the historic Staffordshire district of England, to develop a unique pattern of ironstone dinnerware for the Benjamin Franklin S & L. The result was the blue and white Liberty Blue design that was made exclusively for them.

Fifteen different historic scenes from the American colonial period were used on the dinnerware. The border has a mixture of wild flowers, and a historic scene is in the center of each piece. On the backs, most pieces have a unique backstamp with an eagle holding a flag shield and in the center there is a banner with the words "Original copper engravings of historic colonial scenes printed on Staffordshire Ironstone. Detergent and Dishwasher safe." Above the eagle are the words "Liberty Blue." Directly below the shield are the words "Made in England." Finally, at the bottom, is the name of the scene.

FREE! your lst place setting
by Enoch Wedgwood (Tunstall) Ltd.
for saving at the Benj. Franklin

LIBERTY BLUE
Imported English ★ Ironstone ★

TO COMPLETE YOUR SET: Each time you deposit $50 or qualify for a special discount p either Liberty Blue or Doverst

4-Pc. Place Setting:
1 Dinner Plate, 1 Bread & Butter, 1 Cup, 1 Sau

4 Fruit Dishes
4 Soup/Cereal Dishes
4 Salad Plates
1 Open Vegetable Dish
1 Gravy Boat (2 pieces)
1 Sugar & Creamer
1 12" Platter
1 Covered Casserole
other matching pieces available—see then

Join our 50th Anniversary celebration
and build a set of beautiful dinnerware

FREE with each place setting of Liberty Blue, you will receive a Benj. Franklin commemorative coaster as our 50th Anniversary gift.

To commemorate our 50th year and colonial heritage during this bicentennial period, we are offering this lovely Liberty Blue dinnerware featuring historic American scenes. The pattern is ours alone, made for the Benj. Franklin in Staffordshire, England, famous for its ironstone since 1835. The attractive blue pattern is under glaze, dishwasher-safe and chip resistant.

A 4-piece place setting is yours free with a new deposit of $50 or more. Additional $50 deposits entitle you to purchase extra place settings and accessories at a big discount. We also offer Doverstone for those who prefer a contemporary design. See both patterns on display at your nearby office of the Benj. Franklin.

...or choose **Dovers**

Contempor Stonewar

Offer good ti One free pla account, for only. Dinnere be mailed.

Hillsboro Argus newspaper ad from June 19, 1975
showing initial offering of Liberty Blue.

The dinnerware was advertised as having a hard, fired-on glaze so the color would never fade. The dinnerware was also chip resistant and safe to use in the dishwasher. The blue color was characteristic of the Staffordshire area, where blue had been used for several centuries. It is ironic that this Colonial American design was created in England, since this dinnerware was made to coincide with the American Bicentennial of Independence from England that was celebrated in 1976.

Hillsboro Argus newspaper ad from June 26, 1975 showing first place setting of Liberty Blue could be obtained free with a $50.00 deposit.

LIBERTY BLUE
HISTORIC DINNERWARE

your first place setting FREE!

Now you can build a set of beautiful imported English ironstone by saving at the Benj. Franklin. With a new deposit of $50 or more, your first 4-piece place setting is free. With each subsequent deposit of $50, you may purchase completer units at low cost. See the Liberty Blue display at any of our offices, and start your set today.

Offer good with new deposits only; interest earnings do not qualify. One free gift per family and no mail orders please.

Benj. Franklin
FEDERAL SAVINGS & LOAN ASSN.

Home Office: Franklin Bldg., Portland, Oregon 97204
Robert H. Hazen, Pres. ● 32 Offices ● Phone 248-1234
Hillsboro Office ● 409 East Main Street ● Phone 648-0651
Somerset West Office ● 3300 N.W. 185th Ave. ● Phone 645-4431

The introduction of Liberty Blue was used as a promotion to encourage more deposits with the Benjamin Franklin Federal Savings and Loan. For your first $50.00 deposit, you were given a four-piece place setting free. With every subsequent deposit you could purchase a place setting for only $4.95. As well as this, Benjamin Franklin coasters were given away with each place setting purchased. There were other items that could be purchased at special prices and could be seen on the copy of the original information sheet.

Benjamin Franklin Almanac - July 1975 newsletter from the Benjamin Franklin Savings and Loan showing their 50th anniversary offering.

ALMANAC

A QUARTERLY NEWSLETTER FROM BENJ. FRANKLIN FEDERAL SAVINGS AND LOAN ASSN.
FRANKLIN BUILDING • PORTLAND, OREGON 97204 • 248-1234

LIBERTY BLUE DINNERWARE
Our 50th Anniversary Offer to you

(details page 3)

Liberty Blue dinnerware was made for two years and coincided with the American Bicentennial celebrations. In the October, 1976, issue of the Benjamin Franklin S. & L.'s newsletter, an article was written announcing the end of the promotion. Account holders had only until the end of the year to obtain more Liberty Blue pieces at the special prices offered. This was also an incentive for account holders to continue making additional deposits. In making a $1,000 deposit, one could purchase a forty five piece service for only $45. After December 31st, additional pieces could still be ordered, but they were at a higher cost, from the Sigma Marketing Company in Garden City, New York. In addition, later in 1977, a 20" turkey platter could be obtained free by making a one-time deposit of $5,000.

Article inside the *Benjamin Franklin Almanac* - July, 1975, newsletter describing the Benjamin Franklin Savings and Loan Liberty Blue special offering.

Liberty Blue by Enoch Wedgwood (Tunstall) Ltd.

To commemorate our 50th Anniversary, we looked far and wide for a suitable gift to share with our savers. We chose Liberty Blue dinnerware from Staffordshire, England, famous for ironstone since 1835. The pattern is ours alone, depicting fourteen historic scenes from colonial America. Liberty Blue could become a family heirloom from this bicentennial period. The pattern is protected by a hard fired-on glaze, chip-resistant and dishwasher-safe.

Your first 4-piece place setting is free with a new deposit of $50 or more, and with subsequent $50 deposits you can complete your set at a very low cost.

FREE with each

place setting of Liberty Blue, a Benj. Franklin anniversary coaster.

4-Pc. Place Setting: Dinner Plate, Cup, Saucer, Bread & Butter Plate	$4.95
4 Fruit Dishes	3.95
4 Soup/Cereal Dishes	4.95
4 Salad Plates	4.50
1 Open Vegetable Dish	3.95
1 Gravy Boat (2 pieces)	6.95
1 Sugar & Creamer	8.50
1 12″ Platter	5.95
1 Covered Casserole	9.95
other pieces available — see the display	

Limit 1 free place setting per family, for new deposits only. Transfers from branch to branch and interest earnings do not qualify. Gifts cannot be mailed.

also available contemporary stoneware in sandtone and brown

Doverstone

The Benj. Franklin Celebrates Its 50th Year

Ben H. Hazen
Chairman Emeritus,
Board of Directors.

In 1925, Ben Hazen, now chairman emeritus of the board of directors, met at the Portland Chamber of Commerce with nine local businessmen to plan a new savings and loan association. Among them was Charles F. Berg, who suggested the name "Benj. Franklin" as a symbol of thrift. Frank L. Shull was named the first president, and the original office was opened at the corner of S. W. 4th and Oak with assets of $15,000. In one year, the Benj. Franklin grew to $250,000, and by 1930 it had reached its first $1,000,000.

Early photo of the late Charles F. Berg.

During the bad old days of the great depression a seven-room house with a full basement could be built for under $5,000 — and even that amount was hard to come by. However, the association remained solvent and a passbook was always worth its face value. This was a mark of sound management in a period when many financial institutions were closing their doors.

Then came World War II, when homebuilding gave way to a total defense effort. The end of the war in 1945 released a pent-up demand for housing which gave impetus to the savings and loan industry throughout the nation, and Benj. Franklin was ready with assets of $5,000,000. By 1951, assets totalled $20,000,000, and the first branch office was opened in the Hollywood district. Bob Hazen, Bob Downie and Louis Scherzer opened the new office. Now, 24 years later, they are president and executive vice presidents respectively.

In the ensuing years, the association grew in assets and branch offices. In 1959, Robert H. Hazen was named president and Ben Hazen became chairman of the board. In 1960, assets totalled $100,000,000 and throughout the decade branches were added in greater Portland and in other Oregon cities. By 1971, assets had grown to $400,000,000 and expansion continued including the construction of a number of new offices in the colonial style.

In this golden anniversary year, assets are in excess of $760,000,000, and 31 branches offer the financial resources and services of the Benj. Franklin throughout the state. In a few months, the home office will be moved to the new 19-story Benj. Franklin Plaza at S. W. First and Columbia in downtown Portland, a fitting beginning for our next 50 years.

Benj. Franklin's first office.

Article on back cover of the *Benjamin Franklin Almanac* - July, 1975, newsletter describing the Liberty Blue offer celebrating Benjamin Franklin's 50th year.

Sometime after 1976, the Liberty Blue dinnerware design was released to be sold in national grocery stores on a limited run. The procedure for purchase was similar to that of the Benjamin Franklin. For so many dollar purchases of groceries, you could buy a different piece. Each week there would be a different item to purchase. Additional pieces were made and offered for the grocery store promotions. A guarantee was offered that allowed you to continue purchasing Liberty Blue for five years on an open stock basis from the Sigma Marketing Company. Order blanks were made available for additional pieces after the grocery store promotions ended.

Staff & spouses as shown in an article in the *Benjamin Franklin Almanac* - October 1976 newsletter, letting the Benjamin Franklin Savings and Loan customers know that the special promotion of Liberty Blue was ending on December 31, 1976.

27

Chapter 2

Bowls

Fruit Bowl, 5" diameter, with Betsy Ross Scene

Mrs. Elizabeth Ross, more commonly known as Betsy Ross, was a flag maker for the Pennsylvania Navy, and most likely made the Grand Union flag. According to Betsy's grandson, William Canby, the Continental Congress contacted his grandmother to create a flag for the country in 1776. The story was first told by him in 1870. While Betsy Ross had long been listed as the designer of our flag, it is now felt that several flag makers had an effect on our flag. However, the Betsy Ross story has long been accepted as fact and now is a significant part of our American history and heritage.

On June 14, 1777, Congress passed a bill that officially created a flag for the new country. This flag had thirteen alternating red and white stripes that represented the thirteen original colonies. The dark blue square in the upper left-hand corner contained thirteen white stars that also represented the thirteen colonies. So it was a year after Betsy Ross supposedly designed the flag, that an official style was voted on. Thus, the flag shown in this scene is not historically accurate.

This same scene is found on the covered sugar bowl.

Fruit bowl, 5" diameter with Betsy Ross scene. $13.50

Backstamp on fruit bowl.

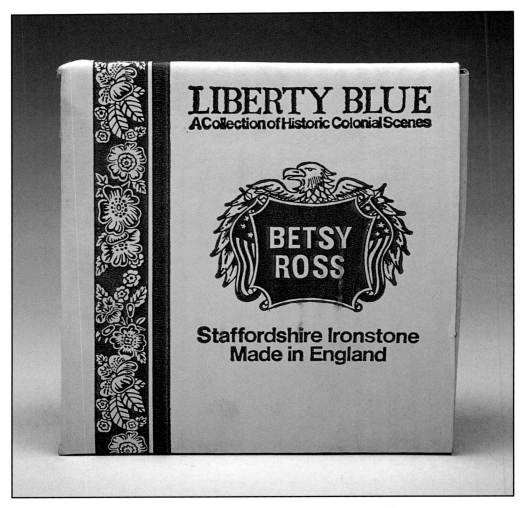

Original box that four fruit bowls were packaged in.

Soup/Cereal Bowl, 6.5" diameter, with Mount Vernon Scene

George Washington's Mount Vernon estate was located in Mount Vernon, Virginia. After inheriting Mount Vernon from a half brother, George Washington made this his home in 1759. Not long after, he married Martha Custis. The house had a spectacular view of the Potomac River and Maryland countryside. The estate was eventually expanded to encompass more than 8,000 acres. Washington set up a grain mill, vineyard, fishery, and beautiful gardens, in addition to the different crops of tobacco and wheat that were grown there.

This same scene is found on the hot chocolate mug.

Soup/Cereal bowl, 6.5" diameter with Mount Vernon scene. $19.50

Backstamp on soup/cereal bowl.

Original box that four soup/cereal bowls were packaged in.

Rim Soup Bowl, 8.75" diameter, with Old North Church Scene

Rim soup bowl, 8.75" diameter with Old North Church scene. $34.50

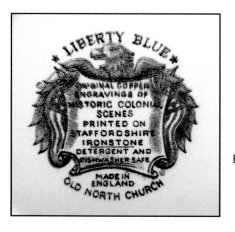

Backstamp on rim soup bowl.

Located in Boston, Massachusetts, construction of this church was completed in 1723. This church was the location of the signal for the start of Paul Revere's famous ride to warn the colonists that the British were coming. At 11pm, on April 18,1775, two lanterns were waved back and forth in the church belfry. This was the signal for Paul Revere, waiting across the river, to start riding on his horse and as he passed through towns he yelled, "To Arms, the British are Coming!"

Today it is Boston's oldest church and contains the original high box pews. A chalice made by Paul Revere is still used during communion there.

This same scene is found on the coaster, milk pitcher, and saucer.

Pattern detail of variant rim on edge of rim soup bowl.

Backstamp on variant rim soup bowl.

Opposite page: Rim soup bowl - variant, 8.75" diameter with Old North Church scene, Note: this one is on a different blank, with a scalloped edge. $39.50

Oval Vegetable Bowl, 9.25" long, with Minutemen Scene

The scene on this piece depicts the Minutemen. These were patriots that were trained to be the militia that would fight for freedom against the British. Minutemen took on this name, because they were expected to be ready on a minute's notice.

This same scene is found cn the soup tureen bottom and teapot.

Oval vegetable bowl, 9.25" long with Minutemen scene. $45.00

Backstamp on oval vegetable bowl.

Round Vegetable Bowl, 8.6" diameter, with Fraunces Tavern Scene

Built in 1719, Fraunces Tavern was located in New York on the corner of Pearl and Broad streets. The Continental Army quietly disbanded in 1783,

Round vegetable bowl, 8.6" diameter with Fraunces Tavern scene. $45.00

Backstamp on round vegetable bowl.

with small groups of men going off in different directions for home. Washington wanted to have a special time to say goodbye to all of his fellow officers. This private celebration took place at Fraunces Tavern. Afterward, Washington headed south, encountering more celebrations all along the way.

Today, the building that housed the Fraunces Tavern is owned by the New York Society of the Sons of the American Revolution. On the upper floors are their offices and a museum with displays about George Washington and the American Revolution. The tavern itself is now leased and operated by a private individual. This scene is found on one of the coasters.

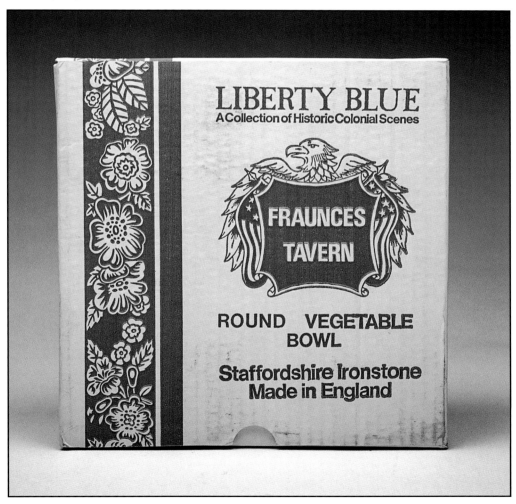

Original box that round vegetable bowl was packaged in.

Round, Covered, Vegetable Bowl, 9.4" diameter, with Boston Tea Party Scene on lid & Lafayette Landing at West Point Scene on bowl

Round, covered vegetable bowl, 9.4" diameter with Boston Tea Party scene on cover and Lafayette Landing at West Point scene on bowl. $145.00

Cover - The Tea Act of 1773 was meant to help the ailing East India Company by selling tea at a cheaper price than could the colonial merchants. The import tea tax still had to be paid though by colonists and they deeply resented this. Finally, the colonists had enough of this unfair taxation. A group of Boston men disguised themselves as native American "Indians" and sneaked aboard the British ships in the harbor. During the night, they dumped

about 10,000 pounds of tea from the ships into the harbor as a retaliation against the unfair tax. Many men so firmly believed this was right, they did nothing to disguise their appearance. Subsequent tea parties also took place in Providence, New York, Greenwich, and Annapolis in 1774.

This same scene is found on the lid of the covered soup tureen cover.

Round covered vegetable shown with lid in an upright position.

Pattern detail of Boston Tea Party scene found on round covered vegetable lid.

Bottom - West Point was a fort located on the Hudson River. It was the center of the line of defense from Morristown to White Plains. Marquis de Lafayette came from a very wealthy family in France. At age 19, he arrived in America on July 27,1777, and volunteered to help the colonists fight the British. Lafayette became very close to Washington, when he joined his staff in August. By the end of the year, he had his own command in the Virginia light infantry. On July 8, 1778, Washington established West Point as his new headquarters.

This same scene is the butter dish and gravy boat.

Pattern detail of Lafayette Landing at West Point scene found on round covered vegetable bowl.

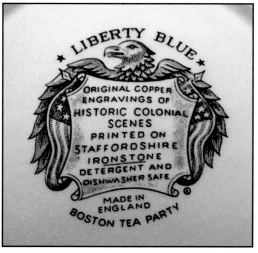

Backstamp on round covered vegetable bowl.

Chapter 3

Butter Dish

**Butter Dish, 8" long, quarter pound, with
Lafayette Landing at West Point Scene**

West Point was a fort located on the Hudson River. It was the center of the line of defense from Morristown to White Plains. Marquis de Lafayette came from a very wealthy family in France. At age nineteen, he arrived in America on July 27, 1777, and volunteered to help the colonists fight the British. Lafayette became very close to Washington when he became part of his staff in August. By the end of the year, he had his own command in the Virginia light infantry. On July 8, 1778, Washington established West Point as his new headquarters.

The same scene is found on the bottom of the covered vegetable bowl and the gravy boat.

Covered rectangle quarter pound butter dish, 8" long with Lafayette Landing at West Point scene. $58.00

Bottom of quarter pound butter dish displayed separately from the lid.

Backstamp on butter dish.

★ LIBERTY BLUE ★

HISTORIC
COLONIAL
SCENES

LAFAYETTE LANDING
AT WEST POINT
MADE IN ENGLAND

Chapter 4

Coasters

Coaster, 4" diameter, with Fraunces Tavern scene

Built in 1719, Fraunces Tavern was located in New York on the corner of Pearl and Broad streets. The Continental Army quietly disbanded in 1783, with small groups of men going off in different directions for home. Washington wanted to have a special time to say goodbye to all of his fellow officers. This private celebration took place at Fraunces Tavern. Afterward, Washington headed south, encountering more celebrations all along the way.

Left - Coaster 4" diameter with Fraunces Tavern scene. $18.00
Right - Coaster 4" diameter with George Washington at Valley Forge scene. $18.00

Today, the building that housed the Fraunces Tavern is owned by the New York Society of the Sons of the American Revolution. On the upper floors are their offices and a museum with displays about George Washington and the American Revolution. The tavern itself is now leased and operated by a private individual.

This same scene is found on the round vegetable bowl.

Coaster 4" diameter, with Washington at Valley Forge scene

At the second meeting of the Continental Congress in June of 1775, John Adams nominated Colonel George Washingtonto be general of all forces. His selection was unanimous. In being a wealthy landowner from Virginia, he refused to accept a salary for his services.

After a long year of fighting in 1777, Washington moved his troops to Valley Forge in October and set up winter camp. Beginning in 1778, the United States and France signed two different treaties. The first was one of allegiance and is the only such one signed in our history. The other treaty was for amity and commerce. With France as our ally, this was a turning point for our fight for independence. With the defeat of Burgoyne, Washington moved out of Valley Forge in June 19, 1778.

Washington's courageous actions inspired men to carry on during the many difficult times of the war. He was elected our first president in 1789 and served for eight years.

The same scene is also found on luncheon plates.

Left - Coaster 4" with Independence Hall scene. $18.00
Right - Coaster 4" with Old North Church scene. $18.00

Coaster, 4" diameter, with Independence Hall scene.

The building was constructed between 1732 and 1756 in brick of Georgian style. Located in Philadelphia, Pennsylvania, it was originally known as the Pennsylvania State House and was also used by the second Continental Congress. Thomas Jefferson wrote the draft of the Declaration of Independence in this building. On July 4, 1776, members of the Congress met and signed the document. The United States Constitution was written here in 1787.

The famous Liberty Bell is housed near this building. During its ringing in 1835 for the funeral of Chief Justice Marshall, the current crack in the bell occurred.

The same scene is found on the dinner plate.

Note: A version of this scene is also found on the Avon decorator plate.

Coaster, 4" diameter, with Old North Church scene

Located in Boston, Massachusetts, construction of this church was completed in 1723. This church was the location of the signal for the start of Paul Revere's famous ride to warn the colonists that the British were coming. At 11pm, on April 18,1775, two lanterns were waved back and forth in the church belfry. This was the signal for Paul Revere, waiting across the river, to start riding on his horse, and as he passed through towns, he yelled, "To Arms, the British are Coming!"

Today it is Boston's oldest church and contains the original high box pews. A chalice made by Paul Revere is still used during communion here.

This same scene is found on the milk pitcher, rim soup, and saucer.

Left - Coaster 4" with Benjamin Franklin. $6.00
Right - Backstamp on Benjamin Franklin coaster.

Coaster, 4" diameter, with Benjamin Franklin scene

This was a premium for account holders at the Benjamin Franklin Federal Savings and Loan. For every place setting purchased, account holders were given this special coaster free to commemorate the 50th anniversary of Benjamin Franklin Federal Savings and Loan. This promotion was done in conjunction with the Bicentennial.

Being from Pennsylvania, Franklin participated in its elections in July, 1776. He was elected President of the Assembly and was also one of the principle writers of the Constitution. Franklin was one of the five members of the drafting committee to write the Declaration of Independence and was one of the signers. He signed the Treaty of Paris in 1782 when Britain formally admitted that the United States was now an independent nation.

Chapter 5

Creamer and Covered Sugar Bowl

Left - Covered sugar bowl, 4.6" tall and holds 12 oz.
Right - Creamer 3.75" tall and holds 11 oz. $65.00 pair

Creamer, 3.75" tall and holds 11 oz., with Paul Revere Scene

The Continental Army was informed about the Massachusetts British governor's plan to arrest John Hancock and Samuel Adams, as well as steal the patriots military stash at Concord. Paul Revere made his famous midnight ride to warn the colonists of the impending attack. At 11pm, on April 18,1775, two lanterns were waved back and forth in the church belfry. This was the signal for Paul Revere, waiting across the river to start his ride. He rode to Medford and Lexington and shouted to every house along the way, "To Arms, the British are Coming!" Paul Revere was actually detained that night by sentries and was not able to complete his ride, since he was not released until morning. What is not commonly known is that there were several other patriots who also rode that night, and at least one of them was a girl.

Revere's lesser-known accomplishments were designing money printing plates for the Massachusetts Congress. He also designed seals for the Massachusetts Congress and for the United States colonies. He was also a well respected silversmith.

This same scene is found on the coffee cup and salt & pepper.

Creamer 3.75" tall with Paul
Revere scene. $30.00

Backstamp on creamer.

Covered Sugar Bowl, 4.6" tall and holds 12 oz., with Betsy Ross Scene

Mrs. Elizabeth Ross, more commonly known as Betsy Ross, was a flag maker for the Pennsylvania Navy, and most likely made the Grand Union flag. According to Betsy's grandson, the Continental Congress contacted his grandmother to create a flag for the country in 1776. The story was first told by him in 1870. While Betsy Ross had long been listed as the designer of our flag, it is now felt that several flag makers had an effect on our flag. However, the Betsy Ross story has long been accepted as fact and now is a significant part of our American history and heritage.

On June 14, 1777, Congress passed a bill that officially created a flag for the new country. This flag had thirteen alternating red and white stripes that represented the thirteen original colonies. The dark blue square in the upper left-hand corner contained thirteen white stars that also represented the thirteen colonies. So it was a year after Betsy Ross supposedly designed the flag, that an official style was voted on. Thus, the flag shown in this scene is not historically accurate.

The covered sugar bowl has the same scene as the 5" fruit bowl.

Backstamp on sugar bowl.

Covered sugar bowl, 4.6" tall with Betsy Ross scene. $35.00

Original box that creamer and sugar bowl were packaged in.

Chapter 6

Coffee Cup and Saucer

Coffee Cup, 2.75" tall and holds 8 oz., with Paul Revere Scene

The Continental army was informed about the Massachusetts British governor's plan to arrest John Hancock and Samuel Adams, as well as steal the patriots' military stash at Concord. Paul Revere made his famous midnight ride to warn the colonists of the impending attack. At 11pm, on April 18,1775, two lanterns were waved back and forth in the church belfry. This was the signal for Paul Revere, waiting across the river to start his ride. He rode to Medford and Lexington and shouted to every house along the way, "To Arms, the British are Coming!" Paul Revere was actually detained that night by sentries and was not able to complete his ride, since he was not released until morning. What is not commonly known is that there were several other patriots who also rode that night, and at least one of them was a girl.

Revere's lesser-known accomplishments were designing money printing plates for the Massachusetts Congress. He also designed seals for the Massachusetts Congress and for the United States colonies. He was also a well respected silversmith.

This same scene is found on the creamer and salt & pepper.

Saucer, 5.75" diameter, with Old North Church Scene

Located in Boston, Massachusetts, construction of this church was completed in 1723. This church was the location of the signal for the start of Paul Revere's famous ride to warn the colonists that the British were coming. At 11pm on April 18,1775, two lanterns were waved back and forth in the

church belfry. This was the signal for Paul Revere, waiting across the river, to start riding on his horse and as he passed through towns, he yelled, "To Arms, the British are Coming!"

Today it is Boston's oldest church and contains the original high box pews. A chalice made by Paul Revere is still used during communion here. The same scene is found on the coaster, milk pitcher, and rim soup bowl.

Left - Saucer for coffee cup, 5.75" diameter with Old North Church scene.
Right - Coffee cup, 2.75" tall and holds 8 oz with Paul Revere scene. $9.50 set

Backstamp on saucer.

Chapter 7
Gravy Boat and Liner

**Gravy boat, 7.75" long, with Lafayette Landing at West Point Scene
and Liner, 7.9" long, with Virginia Governor's House Scene**

Gravy Boat - West Point was a fort located on the Hudson River. It was in the center of the line of defense from Morristown to White Plains. Marquis de Lafayette came from a very wealthy family in France. At age 19, he arrived in America on July 27, 1777, and volunteered to help the colonists fight the British. Lafayette became very close to Washington when he joined his staff in August. By the end of the year, he had his own command in the Virginia light infantry. On July 8, 1778, Washington established West Point as his new headquarters.

This same scene is also found on the bottom of covered vegetable bowl and butter dish.

Gravy boat, 7.75" long. $40.00

Opposite page:
Back - Gravy boat liner, 7.9" long with Governors House scene.
Front - Gravy boat, 7.75" long with Lafayette landing at West Point scene. $65.00 set

Backstamp on gravy boat.

Liner - This mansion was built in 1722 and was home to seven Royal governors of Virginia before the outbreak of the Revolutionary war. Patrick Henry and Thomas Jefferson were the first governors of the Commonwealth of Virginia to reside there. It was used as an official headquarters during the war. Thomas Jefferson started remodeling the house while he lived there. The house was used by American forces as a hospital after the siege of Yorktown. The orchard terrace became a cemetery for fallen patriots.

Backstamp on liner.

Gravy boat liner, 7.9" long. $25.00

In the dead of the night on December 22, 1781, the mansion rapidly burned to the ground in only three hours. For almost 150 years, the grounds were largely ignored. With the restoration of Colonial Williamsburg in the 1920s, the mansion was rebuilt to the original floor plan. The inside was decorated with furnishings that matched its original splendor. On the front of the house, the British royal arms have been rehung above the door to symbolize their importance to the house.

This same scene is also found on the small platter.

Original box that gravy boat and liner were packaged in.

Chapter 8

Hot Chocolate Mug

Hot Chocolate Mug, 3.75" tall and holds 8 oz., with Mount Vernon Scene

George Washington's Mount Vernon estate was located in Mount Vernon, Virginia. After inheriting Mount Vernon from a half brother, George Washington made this his home in 1759. Not long after, he married Martha Custis. The house had a spectacular view of the Potomac River and Maryland countryside. The estate was eventually expanded to encompass more than 8,000 acres. Washington set up a grain mill, vineyard, fishery and beautiful gardens in addition to the different crops of tobacco and wheat that were grown there.

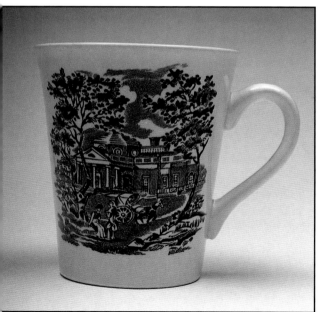

This same scene is also found on the soup/cereal bowl.

Backstamp on hot chocolate mug.

Mug, Hot Chocolate, 3.75" tall and holds 8 oz. with Mount Vernon scene. $18.00

Chapter 9

Name Plates

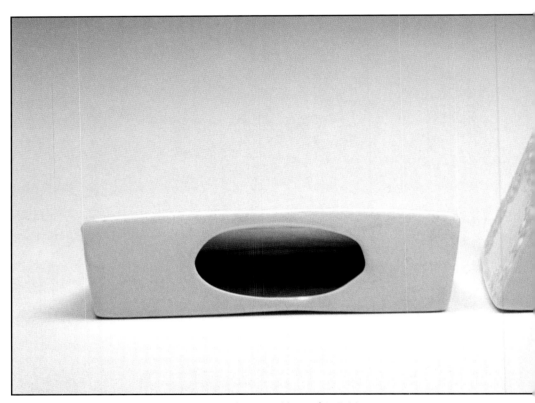

Name plates, 2.25" by 3.75" all white and no markings. $175.00 set
Left - Bottom view
Center - Side View
Right - Front view

These are completely white and do not look like they belong with the Liberty Blue. It is really important to have the original box to identify these. If you are going to purchase them without the original box, then study the photographs of them to make sure that you will recognize them. Embossed at the top is an eagle with its wings spread. The center rectangle area was meant to be used to write your guest's name. There is no mark at all on these and they are easily overlooked.

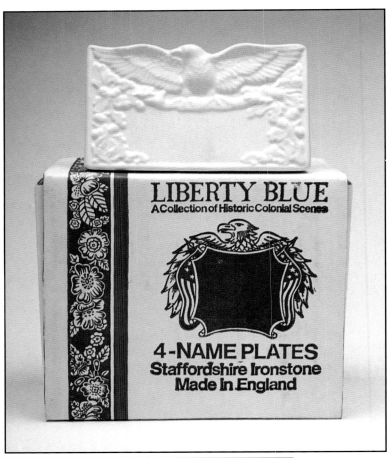

Name plate on top of original box. Four name plates were packaged inside.

"Write your guest's name on the name place card with a magic marker or felt pen. It will wash off and you can use the name place card again, and again, and again."

Original set of instructions enclosed with each set of name plates.

Chapter 10

Milk Pitcher

Milk Pitcher, 7.75" tall and holds 38 oz., with Old North Church Scene

Located in Boston, Massachusetts, construction of this church was completed in 1723. This church was the location of the signal for the start of Paul Revere's famous ride to warn the colonists that the British were coming. At 11pm on April 18,1775, two lanterns were waved back and forth in the church belfry. This was the signal for Paul Revere, waiting across the river, to start riding on his horse and as he passed through towns, he yelled, "To Arms, the British are Coming!" Today, it is Boston's oldest church and contains the original high box pews. A chalice made by Paul Revere is still used during communion here.

The same scene is found on the coaster, rim soup bowl, and saucer. Note: The milk pitcher is often listed as a water pitcher, but there is only one size of pitcher found in the Liberty Blue pattern. We would agree that the use of this pitcher for water makes more sense, however, it is a milk pitcher size.

Milk pitcher, 7.75" tall and holds 38 oz. with Old North
Church scene. $195.00

Backstamp on milk pitcher.

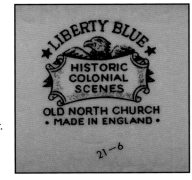

Chapter 11

Plates

Bread and Butter Plate, 5.75" diameter, with Monticello Scene

Thomas Jefferson's plantation was known as Monticello and is located in Albemarle County near Charlottesville, Virginia. Jefferson himself designed his home in a classic Roman style. Built in 1768, it incorporated the many ideas Jefferson had obtained while traveling to Europe. Unlike other southern estates, Jefferson built his house on a leveled hill which hid the surrounding outer buildings. Four white columns provide an outstanding entrance to the home.

Bread and butter plate, 5.75" diameter with Monticello scene. $6.50

Backstamp on bread and butter plate.

Salad Plate, 6.8" diameter, with Washington Leaving Christ Church Scene

The church, located in Alexandria, Virginia, was completed in 1773 and was paid for with tobacco. It was George Washington's home church.

Through the years, this church has had many U. S. presidents and foreign dignitaries attend its services. Today, the church contains Washington's original pew and his family bible.

Salad plate, 6.8" diameter with Washington leaving Christ Church scene. $18.00

Backstamp on salad plate.

Original box that four salad plates were packaged in.

Luncheon Plate, 8.75" diameter, with Washington at Valley Forge Scene

At the second meeting of the Continental Congress in June of 1775, John Adams nominated Colonel George Washington a to be general of all forces. His selection was unanimous. In being a wealthy landowner from Virginia, he refused to accept a salary for his services.

After a long year of fighting in 1777, Washington moved his troops to Valley Forge in October and set up winter camp. Beginning in 1778, the United States and France signed two different treaties. The first was one of allegiance and is the only such one signed in our history. The other treaty was for amity and commerce. With France as our ally, this was a turning point for our fight for independence. With the defeat of Burgoyne, Washington moved out of Valley Forge in June 19, 1778.

Washington's courageous actions inspired men to carry on during the many difficult times of the war. He was elected our first president in 1789 and served for eight years.

The same scene is also found on one of the coasters.

Backstamp on luncheon plate.

Luncheon plate, 8.75" diameter with Washington at Valley Forge scene. $30.00

Dinner Plate, 9.75" diameter, with Independence Hall Scene

The building was constructed between 1732 and 1756 in brick of Georgian style. Located in Philadelphia, Pennsylvania, it was originally known as the Pennsylvania State House and was also used by the second Continental Congress. Thomas Jefferson wrote the draft of the Declaration of Independence in this building. On July 4, 1776, members of the Congress met and signed the document. The United States Constitution was written here in 1787.

The famous Liberty Bell is housed near this building. During its ringing in 1835 for the funeral of Chief Justice Marshall, the current crack in the bell occurred.

This has the same scene as one of the coasters.

Dinner plate, 9.75" diameter with Independence Hall scene. $12.00

Backstamp on dinner plate.

Chapter 12

Platters

Small Oval Platter, 12" long, with Virginia Governor's House Scene

This mansion was built in 1722 and was home to seven Royal governors of Virginia before the outbreak of the Revolutionary war. Patrick Henry and Thomas Jefferson were the first governors of the Commonwealth of Virginia to reside there. It was used as an official headquarters during the war. Thomas Jefferson started remodeling the house while he lived there. The house was used by American forces as a hospital after the siege of Yorktown. The orchard terrace that overlooked the house became a cemetery for fallen patriots.

In the dead of the night on December 22, 1781, the mansion rap-

Backstamp on small size platter.

idly burned to the ground in only three hours. For almost 150 years, the grounds were largely ignored. With the restoration of Colonial Williamsburg in the 1920s, the mansion was rebuilt to the original floor plan. The inside was decorated with furnishings that matched its original splendor. On the front of the house, the British royal arms have been rehung above the door to symbolize their importance to the house.

This same scene is also found on the gravy boat liner.

Small size oval platter 12" long with Governors House scene. $58.00

Medium Oval Platter, 14" long, with Washington Crossing Delaware River Scene

By December 1776, Washington's troops were worn out. Food, supplies and clothing were all a scarce commodity. There was hardly any money to pay the troops. This was a real low point and they needed a miracle to give them encouragement to go on. Washington came up with a brilliant plan. The closest enemy attachment was located in Trenton, New Jersey. On Christ-mas night, Washington knew the enemy would be busy with celebrations. Even though it was a bitter cold night with the wind blowing and snow falling, Washington took this opportunity to move his troops across the Delaware River. By morning they were in position and completely surprised the enemy troops. The battle of Trenton was over in a hour with the capture of 1,000 British troops. This was a major boost for the morale of Washington's men. After this major victory, Congress gave Washington full military powers.

Unfortunately, the scene that was adapted from a famous painting is not historically correct. The actual boats used were Durham Ore boats, not the one depicted in the scene. The Durham Ore boat was a flat cargo boat that resembled a small barge. Also, the flag shown did not exist until after the Flag Act of 1777.

Medium size oval platter, 14" long with Washington crossing Delaware scene. $85.00

Backstamp on medium size platter.

Large Oval Turkey Platter, 20" long, with Signing of the Declaration of Independence Scene

This platter was made only for the account holders at the Benjamin Franklin Federal Savings and Loan. In celebration of the Benjamin Franklin reaching assets of one billion dollars, the Board of Directors offered four special gifts for depositors. One of these gifts was a turkey platter made in Liberty Blue, exclusive to them. The platter was free to people who made a new $5,000 deposit into their account. With a $1,000 deposit, the cost of the platter was $10, and with a $500 deposit the cost was $15. There was a limit of one free gift per account holder and it was only available while supplies lasted. The 20" by 14" platter was only available during the months of October, November and December of 1977. It is assumed that since their contract with Enoch Wedgwood had ended, they choose another manufacturer, since this platter was made in Japan, not England like the previous pieces of Liberty Blue.

The scene on this platter is all the signers of the Declaration of Independence gathered together in a room at Independence Hall. The design was based on an original hand engraving that was inspired by a painting from John Trumbull.

Large size oval turkey platter, 20" long with signing of the Declaration of Independence scene. $225.00

Backstamp on large size turkey platter.

The
Declaration of Independence
1776
From an original hand engraving
inspired by the famous painting
by John Trumbull.

Created for The Benj. Franklin

E DECLARATION OF INDEPENDENCE

Join us in our billion dollar celebration

Excitement is building at The Benj. Franklin as we approach a new milestone of growth. Savings gains have been excellent, and we fully expect assets to reach one billion dollars by the end of this year!

Housing loans are expected to total an all time high of $240 million! Join in the celebration as we look forward to even greater size and strength as Oregon's first billion dollar savings and loan association.

THE DECLARATION OF INDEPENDENCE

See the BIG GIFTS we have FREE for saving now

Huge 20″ x 14″ Turkey Platters

We have some unusual gifts of heirloom quality created exclusively for The Benj. Franklin. Shown above is a 20″ by 14″ turkey platter available in the conventional turkey pattern or the Signing of the Declaration of Independence. FREE for a new deposit of $5,000 or more, or available at low cost with lesser deposit (see chart).

"OUR OREGON" 72 pages of our colorful state

All about colorful Oregon and The Benj. Franklin, this beautiful book features world famous photography of Ray Atkeson. Add to your library or send to friends. FREE while supplies last when you add any amount to your savings account.

Our Oregon

The Un-Candle

Light the floating candle in the tip and decorate lower part for versatile 15″ conversation piece. FREE for a new deposit of $1,000 or only $5 with deposit of $250.

Choose as your gift:	When you open or add to your account with:				
	Any Amount	$250	$500	$1,000	$5,000
Our Oregon book	FREE	FREE	FREE	FREE	FREE
The Un-Candle package	—	$5	$5	FREE	FREE
Independence Platter—blue	—	—	$15	$10	FREE
Turkey Platter—brown	—	—	$15	$10	FREE

The Benj. Franklin

FEDERAL SAVINGS AND LOAN ASSN.
Head Office: Benj. Franklin Plaza • Portland, Oregon 97258
Hillsboro Office • 409 East Main Street • Ph. 648-0651
Somerset West Office • 3300 N.W. 185th Ave. • Ph. 645-4431

Hillsboro Argus newspaper ad from October 4, 1977 showing large size oval turkey platter, 20″ long with signing of the Declaration of Independence scene.

Chapter 13

Shakers

Salt and Pepper Shakers, 3" tall, with Paul Revere Scene

The Continental Army was informed about the Massachusetts British governor's plan to arrest John Hancock and Samuel Adams, as well as steal the patriots' military stash at Concord. Paul Revere made his famous midnight ride to warn the colonists of the impending attack. At 11pm on April 18,1775, two lanterns were waved back and forth in the church belfry. This was the signal for Paul Revere, waiting across the river to start his ride. He rode to Medford and Lexington and shouted to every house along the way, "To Arms, the British are Coming!" Paul Revere was actually detained that night by sentries and was not able to complete his ride, since he was not released until morning. What is not commonly known is that there were several other patriots who also rode that night, and at least one of them was a girl.

Revere's lesser-known accomplishments were designing money printing plates for the Massachusetts Congress. He also designed seals for the Massachusetts Congress and for the United States colonies. He was a well respected silversmith.

This same scene is found on the creamer and coffee cup.

Original box that salts and peppers were packaged in.

Opposite page:
Top: Salt and pepper shakers, 3" tall with Paul Revere scene. $35.00 pair

Bottom: **Left** - Bottom view of shaker.
Right - Upright view of shaker.

Chapter 14

Soup Tureen

Soup tureen with cover, 8″ tall by 13″ wide and holds 112 oz. (3.5 quarts) with Boston Tea Party scene on cover and with Minutemen scene on bottom. $495.00

Soup Tureen with Cover, 8" tall and 13" wide, holds 112 oz. (3.5 quarts), with Boston Tea Party Scene on the lid and Minutemen scene on the bowl

Cover - The Tea Act of 1773 was meant to help the ailing East India Company by selling tea at a cheaper price than could the colonial merchants. The import tea tax still had to be paid though by colonists and they deeply resented this. Finally, the colonists had enough of this unfair taxation. A group of Boston men disguised themselves as native American "Indians" and sneaked aboard the British ships in the harbor. During the night, they dumped about 10,000 pounds of tea from the ships into the harbor as a retaliation against the unfair tax. Many men so firmly believed this was right, they did nothing to disguise their appearance. Subsequent tea parties also took place in Providence, New York, Greenwich, and Annapolis in 1774. The scene is also featured on the covered vegetable bowl cover.

Lid standing upright inside tureen to show pattern.

Opposite page: Pattern detail of Boston Tea Party scene found on soup tureen lid.

Bottom - The scene on this piece depicts the Minutemen. These were patriots who were trained to be the militia that would fight for freedom against the British. Minutemen took this name because they were expected to be ready on a minute's notice.

The same scene is on the oval vegetable bowl and teapot.

Backstamp on soup tureen.

Pattern detail of Minutemen scene found on soup tureen bottom.

Chapter 15

Teapot

Teapot, 6-cup, 6.5" tall and 9" wide, with Minutemen Scene

The scene on this piece depicts the Minutemen. These were patriots who were trained to be the militia that would fight for freedom against the British. Minutemen took this name because they were expected to be ready on a minute's notice.

This same scene is on the oval vegetable bowl and soup tureen bottom.

Backstamp on teapot.

Teapot with lid, 6.5" tall by 9" wide and holds 6 cups with Minute Men scene. $175.00

Original box that teapot and lid were packaged in.

Chapter 16

Go-Along Items

Ladle for Soup Tureens

We could find no evidence that the soup tureen originally came with a ladle. Through the years, people have found ladles that would work well. Johnson Brothers of England has made white ladles to go in their tureens and most people use these with the Liberty Blue tureen. The ladle measures 9" long. It is all white and has no markings on it.

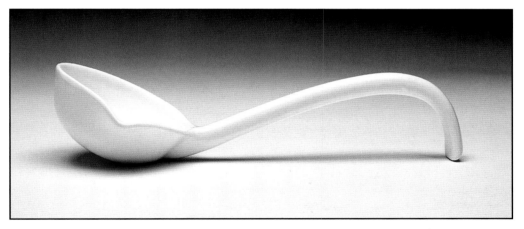

Soup tureen ladle, 9" long all white. Note: this is a Go-Along item. $45.00

Decorator Plates

Enoch Wedgwood designed two plates for the Avon company. Each plate is 7.75" diameter. The blue color and the style was the same as on the Liberty Blue plates. On one plate was the picture of Independence Hall. The other plate depicted the Liberty Bell. Both of the plates were only available to Avon representatives in 1976. Representatives that sent in orders totaling $100.00 or more for Campaigns 1, 2 and 3 were given both plates.

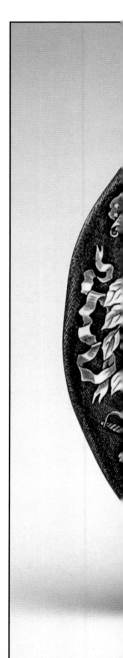

AVON
INDEPENDENCE HALL
BICENTENNIAL PLATE
BIRTHPLACE OF THE DECLARATION OF INDEPENDENCE

Special Edition
Awarded Exclusively to Avon
Representatives.

MADE IN ENGLAND. BY
ENOCH WEDGWOOD (TUNSTALL) LTD.,
© AVON PRODUCTS, INC. 1976.

Backstamp on Avon plate.

Avon decorator plate, 7.75" diameter with Independence Hall scene. Note: this is a Go-Along item. $14.50

Avon decorator plate, 7.75" diameter with Liberty Bell scene. Note: this
is a Go-Along item. $14.50

Backstamp on Avon plate.

Old Williamsburg Stemware

The Old Williamsburg stemware from the Imperial Glass Company was made in an Antique Blue color. This color matches the blue on the Liberty Blue dinnerware very well.

Note: Since no stemware was ever made for Liberty Blue dishes, many collectors are now actively searching for the blue Old Williamsburg stemware.

Imperial Glass Company acquired the molds for this old Heisey pattern in 1958 when the Heisey company closed. Old Williamsburg, line # 341, was a very successful line for the Heisey company and continued to be so for Imperial. This pattern was first reissued in 1959 and continued until 1980 in several different colors. Neither the original Heisey nor the later Imperial pieces were marked. The Antique Blue color was first issued in 1966 and continued until 1975 on some of the stems. A list of the stems made in the Antique Blue color, with the years of production, appears on page 110.

Old Williamsburg stems by Imperial Glass Company. Note: these are Go-Along items.
Left - Claret goblet, 5.25" tall and holds 4.5 oz. $9.50
Left center - Sherbet goblet and holds, 4.75" tall 6 oz. $8.50
Right center - Tall water or table goblet, 6.5" tall and holds 9 oz. $12.50
Right - Footed ice tea tumbler, 6.5" tall and holds 12 oz. $14.50

Goblets:

9 oz	tall goblet	1966-1975
9 oz	low goblet	1972 only
6 oz	tall sherbet	1966-1975
6 oz	low sherbet	1966-1975
4.5 oz	claret	1966-1974
4 oz	wine	1974-1975

Tumblers:

5 oz	flat juice	1971-1976
5 oz	footed juice	1971-1974
8 oz	flat water	1971-1975
12 oz	footed ice tea	1969- 1975
12 oz	footed ice tea	1966-1975
13 oz	double old fashion	1971- 1974

Additionally, there are other go-along glassware pieces that were produced in the Antique Blue color that also make excellent accessory items. All of the following accessory pieces were produced only in 1969:

4.5" compote

9" footed bowl

7" footed covered candy jar

10" footed covered candy jar

10" 3 part relish

13" celery

National Historical Organizations

There are two great national organizations that provide a tremendous amount of information about the American Revolutionary War. Their purpose is to provide historical and patriotic educational information. They also perpetuate the memory of men and women who served during this war to achieve independence of the American people from England. Each of these organizations has state and local chapters that can help in locating information with genealogy of family members who served in the war.

Sons of the American Revolution http://www.sar.org

Daughters of the American Revolution http://www.dar.org

Bibliography

Benjamin Franklin Almanac. Portland, Oregon: Benjamin Franklin Federal Savings & Loan. 1975-1976

Calkins, Carol. *The Story of America.* Pleansantville, New York: Readers Digest Association, Inc., 1975

Colonial Williamsburg Foundation. Official Guide To Colonial Williamsburg. Williamsburg, Virginia: Colonial Williamsburg Foundation. 1990

Commager, Henry Steele. American Destiny Encyclopedia Volume 2&3. United States: Danbury Press. 1976

Cunningham, Jo. *The Best of Collectible Dinnerware.* Atglen, Pennsylvania: Schiffer Publishing, Ltd., 1995

Hastin, Bud. *Avon Products and California Perfume Company Collectibles Encyclopedia.* Kansas City, Missouri: Bud Hastin, 1998

McKinney, W. Verne. *Hillsboro Argus.* Hillsboro, Oregon: Hillsboro Argus Newspaper, 1975-1977

Huxford, Bob & Sharon. *Garage Sale and Flea Market Annual.* Paducah, Kentucky: Schroeder Publishing, 2001

Linton, Calvin. *The Bicentennial Almanac.* New York, New York: Thomas Nelson Inc., 1975

National Imperial Glass Collector's Society. *Imperial Glass Encyclopedia Volume III M-Z.* Marietta, Ohio: The Glass Press, Inc., 1999

Newark Heisey Collectors Club. *Heisey by Imperial.* Newark, Ohio: Heisey Collectors of America, 1982

Readers Digest. *Treasures of America.* Pleasantville, New York: Readers Digest, Inc., 1974

Rinker, Harry. *Dinnerware of the 20th Century: The Top 500 Patterns.* New York, New York: House of Collectibles, 1997

Yaple, Jim. Personal Correspondence. Portland, Oregon: Lewis and Clark Chapter of the Sons of the American Revolution, 2001